PENGUIN BOOKS

HIS HOLINESS THE DALAI LAMA IN 1

Arthy Muthanna Singh is a children's writer, freelance journalist and editor based in Gurugram. She grew up on tea plantations in the Nilgiris. She has authored over thirty books for children and has been helping her mother conduct the Ooty Literary Festival since 2016. She was an editor with *Limca Book of Records* for about thirteen years. She hopes to settle down in Coonoor or Goa someday soon.

Mamta Nainy is a children's writer and editor based in New Delhi. She spent some years in advertising before an apple fell on her head while she was sitting under a mango tree and she had her Eureka moment. She has been writing for children ever since. She has authored many books for children, including *A Brush with Indian Art,* which won The Hindu Young World-Goodbooks Award 2019 for Best Book (Non-Fiction).

PENGUIN BOOKS

USA | Canada | UK | Ireland | Australia
New Zealand | India | South Africa | China

Penguin Books is part of the Penguin Random House group of companies
whose addresses can be found at global.penguinrandomhouse.com

Published by Penguin Random House India Pvt. Ltd
4th Floor, Capital Tower 1, MG Road,
Gurugram 122 002, Haryana, India

First published in Penguin Books by Penguin Random House India 2022

ISBN 9780143454984

Layout and Design by Aniruddha Mukherjee
Typeset in Droid Serif by Syllables27, New Delhi
Printed at Aarvee Promotions, India

www.penguin.co.in

HIS HOLINESS
THE DALAI LAMA IN

100

ANECDOTES

WRITTEN BY ARTHY MUTHANNA SINGH AND MAMTA NAINY

ILLUSTRATIONS BY ANIRUDDHA MUKHERJEE AND CHARULATA MUKHERJEE

INTRODUCTION BY RAJIV MEHROTRA

PENGUIN BOOKS

An imprint of Penguin Random House

INTRODUCTION

'*D*on't be nervous,' I said. 'He's the most human person you could ever hope to meet.'

She gave me a shocked glance. 'He's a living Buddha!' she protested. 'Well, isn't it the same thing?' I asked her.

To the Tibetans, the Dalai Lama is known as *Yeshi Norbu*, the precious wish-fulfilling gem—the reincarnation of Buddha's compassion, Avalokiteshwara. To others, he is known by his Mongol title—the Dalai Lama or 'Ocean of Wisdom'. To the more initiated, he is quite simply, His Holiness. To the millions around the world whose lives he has touched, more often through his ideas than his physical presence, he remains one of the most accessible, self-effacing public figures of the time. His ever-smiling face is a familiar and reassuring presence of the human potential for happiness. We can never completely know and understand the many layers and facets of a human being, less so when that human form is regarded by many as a manifestation of a Buddha, even though he describes himself as a simple Buddhist monk.

What is it that best describes him? At the heart of the man, there seems to exist a profound stillness, even when he engages with the world energetically. His is not a sombre silence but one that brims with joy. His infectious laughter frequently spills over, disarming and moving us all a step closer to our real selves. His is a celestial laugh, which the Tibetans describe as the laugh of the world. The Dalai Lama, even as he embodies the highest aspiration of the Buddhist faith as its preeminent monk, has the courage to be human.

This remarkable book succeeds, as best it conceivably can, in capturing most of the significant anecdotes of an astonishingly rich life. Starting from his childhood in a poor peasant family to his rise as an outstanding spiritual leader, this book is an eventful journey in the life of a statesman who embraced diversity in these troubled times.

Buddha's teaching is a call to the abundance of life and not escapism from an imperfect world. The transient world must end, but humans attain enlightenment and achieve nirvana. To many, the Dalai Lama is more of a god than a mortal. But how does the Dalai Lama want the world to know him? 'Just a human being, perhaps as a human being who smiles?'

Rajiv Mehrotra
May 2022, New Delhi

PREFACE

When we first began our research on His Holiness the Fourteenth Dalai Lama, a phenomenal human being we had long admired from afar, it was almost impossible to remain objective, much as we tried. Speaking to people who have spent time with His Holiness only compounded matters. Most spoke of his compassion and simplicity, many of his sense of humour and childlike chuckle, his twinkling eyes and benign smile when he greets those waiting to meet him. Others spoke of his love for animals, his deep concern for the environment and, of course, that 'special something' that engulfs everyone in his immediate presence—his aura; it's almost impossible to not be inspired and warmed in his rare goodness, they all insisted. What is it about this spiritual leader, who was born in Tibet and lives in exile in India but holds no political position in any country, that makes him so appealing just about everywhere in the world, we wondered.

As we read about his extraordinary life, listened to his talks and went through his interviews, we realized that one of the things that makes His Holiness the best loved spiritual leader of the world is perhaps a deceptively simple—the art of attention and the ability of engaging with everyone with a child's curiosity and a scholar's excitement.

His Holiness makes everyone comfortable by being attentive, listening to each and everything that they have to say. Perhaps this is the reason that people feel at ease in his presence. It is almost like meeting a long-lost friend or a loving family senior and not a spiritual leader or a great philosopher. He does not delve into lofty ideals and long discourses like some know-it-all sage but distills them into everyday, practical wisdom that is simple enough for everyone to understand.

The life of His Holiness is an inspirational song, one that teaches us the importance of interconnectedness and interdependence. It is perhaps not surprising then that during the journey of this book, we learnt a lot—not just about His Holiness but also about our own selves. And we shall forever be grateful for that.

To all of you who read this book, may these lesser-known anecdotes of His Holiness's remarkable life bring you inspiration, joy, warmth, clarity and a little closer to your true self.

Arthy Muthanna Singh and Mamta Nainy

May 2022, New Delhi

'Be kind whenever possible. It is always possible.'

The Previous Lamas

The Dalai Lamas are the highest spiritual leaders of the Tibetan people. His Holiness the Fourteenth Dalai Lama is considered to be the present incarnation of the previous thirteen Dalai Lamas of Tibet (the first having been born in 1391 CE). It is, in fact, believed that he is the seventy-fourth in a lineage that can be traced back to a young boy who lived in the time of the Buddha. Once His Holiness the Fourteenth Dalai Lama was asked if he truly believes in him being an incarnation of the previous lamas. He replied, 'I am often asked whether I truly believe this. The answer is not simple to give. But when I consider my experience during this present life, and given my Buddhist beliefs, I have no difficulty accepting that I am spiritually connected both to the previous Dalai Lamas and to the Buddha himself.'

The Great Thirteenth

At the turn of the twentieth century, China wished to occupy the Tibetan lands. The Thirteenth Dalai Lama, Thubten Gyatso, foresaw that a foreign intervention might threaten Tibet. In 1932, during his last political statement, he made the following prediction: *Very soon in this land deceptive acts may occur from without and within . . . Unless we guard our own country, it will now happen that the Dalai and Panchen Lamas, the father and the son, and all the revered holders of faith, will disappear and become nameless.* Many believe that the Great Thirteenth may have decided that his reincarnation, a younger and stronger Dalai Lama, would be better capable of handling the imminent crisis. So, he designed the time of his death as *boddhisattvas*, or individuals who are on the path to becoming a Buddha, are believed to be able to do. On 17 December 1933, he died at the age of fifty-eight.

3

Signs of a Rebirth

Grieving Tibetans were preparing for the funeral of the departed Dalai Lama. His body was mummified and dressed in a brocade robe. He was seated on the throne in the Norbulingka Palace, the summer palace of the Dalai Lama. It was around this time that the first clues of Dalai Lama's incarnation arose. The first sign was the turning of the Dalai Lama's head, which had been faced southwards. But overnight, his head was discovered to have turned from facing south to the north-east. It was repositioned, but the next day, it was again found facing eastwards. This was taken to be a sign that the next Dalai Lama would hail from the east. There were a few other signs, too, that pointed in the direction of a possible reincarnation: On one of the pillars of the tomb of the Thirteenth Dalai Lama, which was under construction at Potala Palace, the winter palace of the Dalai Lama, a star-shaped fungus appeared. Cloud formations in the shapes of elephants were also spotted in the north-eastern skies.

The Regent's Vision

Following the reported signs, the Tibetan officials decided to appoint a regent, a senior lama who is chosen to rule the country until the next Dalai Lama reaches full maturity to rule alone. One of the primary responsibilities of the regent was to find the Dalai Lama's reincarnation. The regent, Reting Rinpoche, travelled to the sacred lake of Lhamo Lhatso, also called the Oracle Lake, in southern Lhasa. Visions from the lake had led to the discovery of the Thirteenth Dalai Lama and so the regent hoped that he would have a vision there, too. He went into deep meditation. When he opened his eyes, he saw the Tibetan letters *Ah*, *Ka* and *Ma* floating into view. These were followed by the image of a three-storeyed monastery. Finally, he saw a house with a turquoise-tiled roof and juniper guttering. He was sure that the letter *Ah* referred to Amdo, Tibet's north-eastern province, and decided to send a search party there.

5

Born Lhamo Thondup

Meanwhile, on 6 July 1935, in the small village of Taktser, located in the province of Amdo, a baby was born to a peasant couple. Taktser, or 'roaring tiger' in Tibetan, stood on a hill, overlooking a broad valley. There were only about twenty families living in the village, since the wide pastures of the village were tough to farm. The baby's birth was auspicious for his family, as his father recovered from a fatal illness soon after his birth. He was named Lhamo Thondup, which means 'the wish-fulfilling goddess' in Tibetan. At the time of Lhamo's birth, his eldest sister, who was about eighteen at that time, acted as the midwife. When the baby was delivered, she noticed that one of his eyes was wide open and he did not cry. Without hesitation, she put her thumb on the reluctant lid and forced it open, fortunately without harming the baby.

The Crow Connection

Just after Lhamo was born, his mother noticed a pair of crows roosting on the roof of their home. She did not take any notice of them in the beginning, but then they would arrive every morning. Similar incidents had taken place after the births of the First, Seventh, Eighth and Twelfth Dalai Lamas as well. In fact, after the birth of the First Dalai Lama, bandits had broken into the family's house and the parents had run away in fright, leaving the child behind. When they returned the next day, they found a crow perched before the baby. Much later, the First Dalai Lama made direct contact with the protective deity Mahakala during meditation. At this time, Mahakala said to him, 'Somebody like you, who is upholding the Buddhist teachings, needs a protector like me. Right on the day of your birth, I helped you.' So, the Tibetan Buddhists believe that there is a connection between the protective Mahakala, the crows and the Dalai Lamas.

7

A Family of Lamas

Lhamo's mother gave birth to sixteen children, of whom only seven survived. Lhamo had two sisters and four brothers. His eldest brother, Jigme Norbu, was recognized as the reincarnation of a high lama, Taktser Rinpoche. His second brother, Gyalo Thondup, became sick soon after birth. His father invited the oracle (a priest who makes prophetic predictions) from the monastery to bless his infant son. When the oracle visited their home, he went into a sudden trance. The father fell to his knees, saying, 'I have lost three sons already and now the fourth one is sick too. Please accept him as your adopted son and keep him away from harm.' The oracle agreed and, from that time on, the child was never sick. So, when Lhamo's parents had another son a few years later, they decided that he should be a monk. He was the immediate elder brother of Lhamo, Lobsang Samten. At six, he joined the Kumbum Monastery. The youngest brother, Tenzin Choegyal, was also recognized as the reincarnation of a high lama, Ngari Rinpoche.

An Unusual Toddler

Right from the time Lhamo was born, he showed some unusual behaviour. As a toddler, he demanded his father's seat at the head of the table. He would allow only his mother to serve him food. He disliked quarrelsome people, and when he was a year old, he tried to attack the offenders with sticks. Young Lhamo also seemed to be obsessed with Lhasa, Tibet's capital. He would pack his things in a bag as if he was about to go on a long journey. He would then straddle a windowsill, pretending that he was on horseback and exclaim, 'I'm going to Lhasa! I'm going to Lhasa!' He also enjoyed going into the chicken coop to collect eggs with his mother. He would then stay behind. He sat there, making clucking noises. But, for the most part, Lhamo's parents didn't take much notice of the child's eccentricities.

9

The Search Parties

When the regent came back to Lhasa, he reported his vision to the government. After consulting state oracles, three search parties were put together of the closest monastic attendants of the Thirteenth Dalai Lama and sent to different parts of eastern Tibet. The members of the search parties disguised themselves to prevent any manipulation of the process. One party, headed by Kewtsang Rinpoche of the Sera Monastery, made its way to Amdo in the far north-east region of Tibet. He was given several objects that belonged to the Thirteenth Dalai Lama to test candidates for the reincarnation. The party travelled for many days and arrived at the home of the second most important lama in Tibet, the Panchen Lama. The lama gave them a list of three boys who might be the potential candidates. They all lived near the Kumbum Monastery, which had a jade-and-gold roof and fitted the regent's vision perfectly. The party was now convinced that the Tibetan letter *Ka* referred to the Kumbum Monastery.

Divine Intervention

The search party headed by Kewtsang Rinpoche then proceeded to look for the first potential candidate. When they reached his home, they found that the boy had died. When they went to the house of the second candidate, the child ran away from them—which, according to them, was quite an odd behavior for a potential Dalai Lama. When they started walking towards the house of the third candidate, they found themselves at a fork in the hilly path. Just then, they met a Chinese boy who advised them to take the lower road. They saw it as divine intervention as, when they took the lower road and looked down, they saw a small house in the distance. It had turquoise tiles trimming its roof and juniper guttering—resembling exactly the vision of the regent!

11

The First Sign

The search party had disguised themselves as a group of travellers. It was a common practice in Tibet for travellers to stay in the houses of native people because of the lack of hotels and guest houses. Little Lhamo was delighted to see Kewtsang Rinpoche, who was disguised as a servant. He settled on Rinpoche's lap. The rosary around his neck caught Lhamo's fancy and he reached for it. The lama told the child that the rosary was old and he would give him a new one. But the child continued to demand the rosary. 'I will give it to you,' said Kewtsang Rinpoche finally, 'if you tell me who I am.' 'You are Sera-lama,' replied Lhamo. 'An elder from the Sera Monastery.' The lama was shocked. One by one, Lhamo identified all his colleagues correctly. Kewtsang Rinpoche spent most of the day observing the little boy, who seemed very attached to the rosary that belonged to the Thirteenth Dalai Lama. The next morning, the search party left and, to his mother's surprise, Lhamo ran after them, crying that he wanted to go with them too.

The Three Tests

The monks were excited that Lhamo had passed the first test. But they had to be sure. A few weeks later, they came back without disguises. They laid out two rosaries in front of Lhamo and asked him to choose one. He chose the one that belonged to the Thirteenth Dalai Lama. Next, he was showed two small religious drums. One was made of simple ivory and the other, more ornate. Yet Lhamo chose the simple one—the correct one. Finally, he was asked to choose between two walking sticks—the first one was Rinpoche's and the other one belonged to the Thirteenth Dalai Lama. Lhamo put his hands on both the sticks and then pulled one hand away, choosing the correct stick. The first stick was given to Rinpoche by the Thirteenth Dalai Lama and that explained the initial uncertainty of the child. The monks bowed down to Lhamo, exclaiming, '*Kundun*—the presence of the Buddha!' Their search for the Fourteenth Dalai Lama was over!

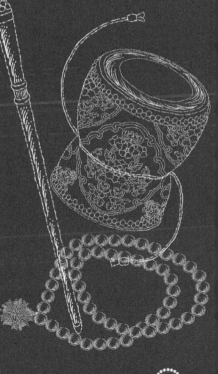

13 Ransom for Young Lhamo

While arrangements were being made to take Lhamo to Lhasa, nobody foresaw an obstacle. Amdo was under the powerful Chinese warlord, Ma Bufang. He had not been informed that the Dalai Lama's incarnation had been found. Instead, the search party had told him that they were in Amdo to look for suitable candidates and Lhamo was the most likely one. Ma Bufang demanded an enormous ransom from the Tibetan government to allow the child and his family to leave Amdo. When the payment was made, he demanded more. After being recognized as a reincarnated Dalai Lama, Lhamo couldn't continue living at his home. So, he was brought to the Kumbum Monastery and had to stay there under the care of his uncle. The Dalai Lama describes his initial period at the Kumbum Monastery as 'a somewhat unhappy period of my life'. However, there were two consolations for him—his elder brother Lobsang Samten was with him and his teacher was a very kind old monk. For about eighteen months, Lhamo stayed on in Amdo until the negotiations were finalized.

The Mixed-up Scriptures

At the Kumbum Monastery, little Lhamo and his brother Lobsang got into mischief ever so often. Once, Lhamo found a set of palm-leaf scriptures and mixed them all up. When his uncle found out, he was mad at the boy and slapped him hard. But there were occasions when Lhamo and Lobsang managed to save themselves from their uncle's wrath by hiding from him for hours. From under the cot, they could hear their uncle getting angrier and angrier, but they wouldn't come out. They were both too young to understand the responsibility that their uncle was shouldering. Ensuring the secrecy and the safety of the Fourteenth Dalai Lama was not an easy task, after all.

15

At Long Last

After eighteen months of negotiations between the Tibetan government and Ma Bufang, the matter was finally resolved and Lhamo was allowed to travel to Lhasa. A group of wealthy Muslims were going to a pilgrimage to Mecca through India, and they agreed to escort the boy to Lhasa. The journey from Amdo to Lhasa began in July 1939. Lhamo was reunited with his family as they accompanied him on the journey that took three months and thirteen days. The entourage also included monks, pilgrims, Muslim escorts and guides on over 350 horses and mules. Lhamo, along with his brother Lobsang Samten, travelled in a special carriage that was strapped on two mules. Since there were no proper roads, the journey was arduous. So, the group travelled from morning to noon. Little Lhamo looked at everything on his journey with a great sense of wonder—yaks grazing across the plains, wild asses breaking into a run, flocks of hooting geese and the super elusive deer called *gowa* and *nawa*.

The Forbidden City, Finally!

When the travelling party had safely crossed the Chinese control, a formal declaration was made by the Tibetan government that the Fourteenth Dalai Lama had been found. After spending three months on the road, Lhamo and his entourage were received by the first welcoming party at the Thotupchu River. The welcoming party had brought along with them some supplies and four yak-skinned boats (or coracles) to take them across the river. Another party that included the oracle priest of Tibet, a monk from the Drepung Monastery and a minister welcomed the Dalai Lama. Lhamo's parents were bestowed the titles *Gyalyum* (the great mother) and *Gyalyap* (the great father). His father was offered the fancy clothes of a minister and his mother was offered dresses and jewellery worn by royal women. While Lhamo's father wore the clothing given to him, his mother preferred wearing her own clothes and said that she would be more comfortable in what she was used to wearing.

17

From Lhamo to Lama

Lhamo was dressed in a yellow brocade robe and a yellow fur hat—yellow being the colour used only by the Dalai Lamas. He was transferred to a golden palanquin. Monks carrying big banners led the procession. Behind Lhamo was a monk bearing a huge umbrella of peacock feathers. The fragrance of incense wafted through the air as the majestic procession advanced to the sound of trumpets. The procession stopped when it reached Doguthang Plain, a few kilometres away from the gates of the capital. The four-year-old Lhamo was taken into a tent called the Great Peacock, previously owned by the Thirteenth Dalai Lama. He was made to sit on a carved wooden throne, used especially to welcome baby Dalai Lamas. He was also given a yellow tassel, with which he blessed the leading monastic officials who passed before him. The small boy's dignity and patience impressed everybody; he seemed completely at ease with his new life. From Lhamo, he transformed into Kundun or the presence of the Buddha.

The Grand Procession

A couple of days later, the grand procession continued from the Doguthang Plain into the city of Lhasa, towards Norbulingka Palace. Nobles dressed in satin robes and tasseled hats carried the new Dalai Lama in his golden palanquin. Monks and ministers, officials and administrators, astrologers and doctors, Lhamo's family and well-wishers—all joined the procession. The band of the Tibetan army played 'God Save the King', which they'd learned during the reign of the Thirteenth Dalai Lama. The route was crowded with thousands of peasants bowing their heads in honour of the new Dalai Lama. They were all dressed in their best clothes and wore all the jewellery they owned. The windows of all the houses were shut as no one could look at the Dalai Lama from above. More people joined the procession on the way, before it finally reached Norbulingka, which was to be the Dalai Lama's home until his final enthronement at Potala Palace.

19

The Summer Residence

When the procession reached the Norbulingka Palace on 8 October 1939, all the travellers were treated to a welcome party with a high tea. After the party, the Dalai Lama was directed to his quarters and his family to theirs. Surrounding the Norbulingka were two sets of yellow walls. The inner wall marked the area where only the Dalai Lama and his attendants were allowed. His family and officials lived between the inner and the outer walls. The eastern half of the palace premises included the palace section, the opera and government offices. The palace section held two palaces and the opera grounds had an open theatre and lush gardens, where the Opera Festival was held every year. There was also a big courtyard where debates were held. But the most beautiful of all these areas was the Lake Palace complex. In the centre of the lake were three islands, on each of which stood a palace. The islands were connected to each other with short bridges.

The Lost Treasure

As soon as Lhamo reached his quarters, he started looking for something desperately. He searched every nook and cranny and had all the sealed trunks and boxes opened, one after the other. He stated again and again that he was looking for a box in which he had stored his teeth. And finally, he found what he was looking for! Spotting a small box wrapped in a brocade cloth, he cried out excitedly, 'This box contains my teeth!' The box was opened to reveal that it did in fact contain a set of dentures thatbelonged to the Thirteenth Dalai Lama.

21

Lhamo's Favourite Attendant

The Dalai Lama was given three attendants who were all monks—The Master of the Ritual, the Master of the Kitchen and the Master of the Robes. The Master of the Kitchen was Dalai Lama's favourite as he had formed a unique bond with him. He called him 'Ponpo' and didn't let the man out of his sight even for a second. His presence provided him a sense of comfort. Even a glimpse of the hem of his robe behind a closed door was enough for the little boy. He felt quite relieved knowing that he was around. Once, while talking about his endearing bond with Ponpo, the Dalai Lama said, 'I sometimes think that the act of bringing food is one of the basic roots of all relationships.'

Days at Norbulingka

Little Lhamo loved the many different trees in Norbulingka Palace. The gardens were filled with juniper, apple, pear, peach, walnut and apricot trees, and Lhamo would pick and savour the fruits of these trees. The palace had huge empty spaces to play and run around. It also had many lakes and ponds. Lhamo was interested in boating. He and his brother often fished in the pond with a fishing net, but they always released the fish they caught. The fish were more like their pets. When they went boating, the fish would often rise to the surface at the sound of the oar, asking to be fed.

23

A Thousand-roomed Palace

After staying for four months in Nobulingka Palace, on 22 February 1940, the Dalai Lama was taken to Potala Palace, the largest structure in Tibet with over 1,30,000 square metres of interior space and a thousand rooms, for his official enthronement. Set high on the great Tibetan plateau, against the looming backdrop of the Himalayas, the vast structure rose 400 feet from a mountain in the middle of Lhasa, making the uppermost apartments on its thirteenth floor 12,500 feet above sea level. Here, preparations had begun months in advance and many dignitaries from foreign countries were invited for the Dalai Lama's enthronement ceremony, which was to be held in the Hall of All Good Deeds of the Spiritual and Temporal Worlds.

The Enthronement Ceremony

Upon his arrival, the Dalai Lama was seated on the Lion Throne. Supported by eight snow lions, the national symbol of Tibet, the wooden throne was encrusted in various jewels and precious stones. The Dalai Lama's enthronement ceremony opened with the regent presenting him the *Mendel Tensum*, a traditional offering that consisted of a golden figure of the Buddha, a book of scriptures about the Buddha and a miniature container containing a holy relic. He was also presented the Golden Wheel and the White Conch as symbols of spiritual power. Various officials offered ceremonial scarves called *khatags* to the new Dalai Lama and the other guests offered him good wishes and gifts. Mime and music performances were staged to entertain the audience. The entire ceremony lasted for over five hours, but not once did the young Dalai Lama fidget, like any other four-year-old would.

25

Tenzin Gyatso, the Fourteenth Dalai Lama

After the enthronement ceremony, the Dalai Lama and his brother Lobsang Samten were taken to the Jokhang Temple and were initiated as monks. Their heads were shaved and their names changed by the regent. Lhamo Thondup was given the name Jamphel Ngawang Lobsang Yeshe Tenzin Gyatso, meaning 'The holy lord, gentle glory, the compassionate one, defender of the faith, ocean of wisdom'. His official signature would be Tenzin Gyatso, the Fourteenth Dalai Lama.

The Best Gift

The dignitaries and foreign representatives who attended the coronation ceremony had brought a number of gifts for the new Dalai Lama. Among them were gold, silver, precious stones, horses, cattle, rare manuscripts, a six-foot elephant tusk, a gold watch and chain, rolls of brocade, etc. But the young Dalai Lama looked at all of them indifferently until one gift caught his fancy. A British representative had brought him a model construction toy set from the famous mechanical toy company, Mecanno, which had an assortment of reusable metal strips, wheels, axles and nuts and bolts. His favourite pastime was now, taking the machines apart to see how they worked and putting them together again. So, it was the perfect gift for the young Dalai Lama.

27

Lhamo's Friends

Lhamo's only friends were his attendants. Although they were all much older than him, they played with him. One of the games they played often was a game where they would place a flower or a stone or a cookie some distance away and then race to see who would get it first. When they used a flower, they would say, 'Oh, let His Holiness win . . .' and would allow little Tenzin to get the flower. But when they used a cookie, they would all run fast and not allow His Holiness to win it at all.

A Small Saviour

The naughty Lhamo, now Tenzin Gyatso, began to live in Potala Palace—a huge, dark, cold palace that little Tenzin sometimes found scary. There were many murals of previous Dalai Lamas and various deities in the palace. To the young Dalai Lama, they sometimes looked scary, especially at night. His only saviour was a little mouse who would come down to drink butter from the butter lamps each night. The child felt very happy when he saw the mouse. It brought him instant comfort.

The Three Tutors

Despite his tender age of six, the Dalai Lama was put through the rigorous training of the traditional Tibetan monastic studies. He had three tutors. He had a great liking for both his main teachers, Ling Rinpoche and Trijang Rinpoche. But he was most attached to his third tutor—who was none other than Kewtsang Rinpoche, the leader of the search party who identified him as a reincarnation of the Great Thirteenth. The Dalai Lama, however, took advantage of his affection sometimes, by insisting that his tutor recite the lessons himself!

A Reluctant Student

Much like most children, the young Dalai Lama's days were often filled with aversion to studies. In the classroom, His Holiness recalls, the Master of Ritual would sometimes nod off while reciting the morning prayers. This would give him the opportunity to look outside the window at the chirping birds perched on a big tree. The Dalai Lama describes how the Master's voice would sound like a gramophone record slowing down as he fell asleep—only to wake up with a start. Having lost his train of thought, the confused teacher would then start the prayers all over again!

31

Love for Science

As a young boy, the Dalai Lama became hugely interested in science and technology. Whenever he got a toy, he would play with it for a while, but soon take it apart to see how it was put together. One of his favourite toys was a train set and some toy soldiers. He melted many of his toy soldiers only to recast them as monks. He enjoyed repairing watches too. Over the span of several decades, the Dalai Lama has met leading scientists, Nobel Prize winners, and experts in cosmology, neuroscience, quantum physics and psychology. The Dalai Lama describes himself as, 'My body, this person, half Buddhist monk, half scientist.'

Telescope Sessions

At one point the Dalai Lama came across an old brass telescope that belonged to the Thirteenth Dalai Lama. With this telescope he would gaze from the Potala Palace's roof at Lhasa's street life. Through this telescope, he would also study the heavens. One night, while looking at the moon, he realized that there were shadows on its surface. He quickly called his two main tutors to show them. This was contrary to the ancient version of cosmology, which believed that the moon was a heavenly body that emitted its own light. But through his telescope, he could see that the moon was clearly just a barren rock, scarred with craters. And the shadows on the moon were proof that the moon was lit by the sun's light, in the same way the earth is.

33 Driving a Car

In the mid-1920s, Sir Charles Albert Bell, the trusted British political agent for Tibet, had presented a Baby Austin A-40 car that carried the licence plate TIBET 1 to the Thirteenth Dalai Lama. This car was probably one of three cars that belonged to the Thirteenth Dalai Lama. As a young boy, the Fourteenth Dalai Lama pulled out parts from it, with the help of the previous Dalai Lama's driver, to get a twenty-year-old Dodge car running again. It was not long before he took that car out for a ride in the gardens of Norbulingka Palace, urging the driver not to tell anyone about it.

A Gift from President Roosevelt

The Dalai Lama has long had a fascination with watches. In 1942, two agents from the Office of Strategic Services (the predecessor of Central Intelligence Agency) presented the Dalai Lama with a handwritten letter and a special gift from the US president Franklin Delano Roosevelt—a Patek Philippe gold chronograph watch. These two intelligence agents, Captain Brooke Dolan, an experienced American explorer, and Major Ilia Tolstoy, the grandson of Russian novelist Leo Tolstoy, were visiting Lhasa on a first-of-its-kind mission to discover routes to China that cut through India and Tibet, in order to transport supplies to China to fight the Japanese as the world's powers battled in World War II. Though the young Dalai Lama cared little about the letter from the US President, he was delighted on receiving the watch.

35

The Austrian Influence

Heinrich Harrer was an Austrian mountaineer who fled a British prisoner of war camp in India to the northern Himalayas. He, along with the expedition leader Peter Aufschnaiter, spent nearly two years crossing the Himalayas by foot, traversing about fifty mountain passes more than 5000 metres high. The pair reached Tibet's capital city, Lhasa, on 15 January 1946. Visitors from outside Tibet were very rare in those days. Harrer met the Fourteenth Dalai Lama, then about thirteen years of age. When he was summoned to Potala Palace, he was asked to make a film about ice skating, which Harrer had introduced in Tibet. In 1948, he was invited to become a salaried official of the Tibetan government, as a translator of foreign news and the court photographer of the young Dalai Lama.

The Film Projector

The Dalai Lama had a movie projector that belonged to the Thirteenth Dalai Lama. However, it did not work properly. So Harrer was called one day to fix it. He not only fixed the projector but also built a screening room in Norbulingka Palace with a generator shed. The adolescent Dalai Lama was utterly pleased with this. He asked Harrer many questions about the functioning of the projector and helped him load the reels of a documentary on Japan's defeat in World War II. After the screening, the Dalai Lama told Harrer that he wished to learn things beyond his religious instruction. Harrer soon became one of the Dalai Lama's tutors and introduced many scientific ideas to him. In 1950, Harrer returned to Austria and documented his experiences in two books—*Seven Years in Tibet* (1952) and *Lost Lhasa* (1953). In October 2002, the Dalai Lama presented Harrer with the International Campaign for Tibet's Light of Truth Award, for his efforts in bringing the tragic situation in Tibet to international attention.

37 China Lays an Evil Plot

In the year 1950, on the orders of Mao Zedong, the supreme leader of the Communist Party of China, Chinese forces began to attack Tibet with an agenda to eventually invade it. Over 80,000 Chinese soldiers had been deployed along Tibet's borders. When the Tibetans heard about the advancing troops, they were in complete shock. On 7 October 1950, the Chinese forces invaded Tibet at six different places at the same time. The Tibetan Army tried to fight back bravely but were ill-prepared to defend themselves. Since Tibet had largely been an independent state, it lacked modern weapons, trained armies and paved roads. The Tibetans were, therefore, outnumbered and defeated. Chamdo was taken over and fear spread through Lhasa. 'Had the country modernized earlier instead of shunning reforms,' the Dalai Lama later wrote, 'I am quite certain that Tibet's situation today would be very different.'

A Head of State at Fifteen

With the growing aggression of the Communist Chinese, the need to enthrone the Dalai Lama earlier than scheduled kept growing. The Tibetan people needed a political leader. At this time the Dalai Lama was visited by his elder brother, Taktser Rinpoche, who was the lama of the Kumbum Monastery in Amdo. His anguished tales of the cruel occupation of the Chinese and the torture many fellow Tibetans had to undergo moved the Dalai Lama deeply. His brother tried to persuade him to go into exile. But the Dalai Lama would not. Instead, at just fifteen years of age, three years before his slated time, he officially assumed the role of the political and the spiritual leader of Tibet in a special ceremony held at Norbulingka Palace on 17 November 1950. By this time, the Chinese had occupied two-thirds of Tibet. To thwart any kind of security threat, the Dalai Lama and his family temporarily moved to Dromo, near the Indian frontier.

39 The Seventeen-Point Agreement

In May 1951, under pressure from the Chinese, the Tibetan government sent a delegation headed by Ngapo Jigme, the Governor of Chamdo, to negotiate with the Chinese in Beijing. Under duress, Ngapo signed the Seventeen-Point Agreement for the Peaceful Liberation of Tibet on 23 May 1951 between Lhasa and Beijing. As the Dalai Lama listened to the radio broadcast one morning, 'a harsh, crackling voice announced that a Seventeen-Point Agreement for the Peaceful Liberation of Tibet had been signed by the representatives of the government of the People's Republic of China and what they called the "Local Government" of Tibet.' The Dalai Lama had kept all the official seals with him in Dromo so that no one could sign any treaty without his consent. But the Chinese got duplicate seals made and threatened military action against Lhasa, forcing Ngapo Jigme to sign the agreement. The Dalai Lama felt 'physically ill after listening to this unbelievable mixture of lies', he later recalled, as the treaty was absolutely detrimental to Tibet's sovereignty. But there was nothing he could do. It was too late.

A Trip to Beijing

The situation in Tibet kept getting worse. Very few people outside Tibet really knew what was actually happening in that distant land. By the time the Dalai Lama returned to Lhasa in August 1951, his followers were very relieved. They never wanted him to leave Lhasa again. However, in his absence, friction between the Tibetan Prime Minister Sitsab Lukhangwa and the Chinese representative, General Zhang Jingwu, had become frequent. The Dalai Lama was forced to intervene. He realized that he would have to be the only one to have interactions with the Chinese. So, in June 1954, when the Chinese invited him to attend the People's National Assembly, he decided to visit Beijing. Many people tried to dissuade him, but the Dalai Lama thought it was an excellent opportunity. Not only would he meet Chairman Mao in person but also give him an opportunity to see another world beyond his homeland. With a delegation of over 400 officials, monks and Tibetan elite, the Dalai Lama left for Beijing.

41

Meeting Mao

A week after his arrival in Beijing, the Dalai Lama met Chairman Mao. The first meeting was quite a success. The Dalai Lama felt 'he was in the presence of a magnetic force' as he shook hands with Mao, who greeted him as though he were an old friend. Mao spoke well of Tibetan people and told the Dalai Lama that the reforms would be carried out according to their wishes. Despite many apprehensions, the Dalai Lama felt positive about his visit. Several meetings followed after that and, towards the end of his year-long visit, the Dalai Lama hosted a banquet for Mao. Prior to his departure, the Dalai Lama had a final appointment with Mao. 'Your attitude is good,' Mao said. 'But religion is poison. Firstly, it reduces the population because monks and nuns remain celibate and secondly, it neglects material progress.' The Dalai Lama was shocked by how wrongly Mao had judged him. He had misinterpreted his interest in scientific and material progress, in his own ignorance of the Buddhist philosophy. The Dalai Lama, however, concealed his feelings.

First Visit to India

In 1956, the Dalai Lama travelled to India upon the invitation of Indian Prime Minister Jawaharlal Nehru and the crown prince of Sikkim, Palden Thondup Namgyal, who was also the president of the Mahabodhi Society. The Dalai Lama was to participate in the celebration of the 2500th anniversary of the Buddha's Enlightenment. Travelling first by car via Shigatse, where he was joined by the Panchen Lama, the Dalai Lama spent a short time at Dromo, the small town on the Indo-Tibetan border that he had last seen in 1951. He then continued his journey on horseback, up the steep track that led to the Nathula Pass and reached Sikkim on the other side. A grand ceremony was arranged by the chogyal (or king) of Sikkim, Tashi Namgyal, to welcome the Dalai Lama in Gangtok.

43

Visit to Rajghat

The Dalai Lama flew to Delhi from Bagdogra. He was met by Prime Minister Jawaharlal Nehru at the airfield. His very first engagement was to lay flowers and a *khatag* at Rajghat on the banks of the Yamuna River, in honour of Mahatma Gandhi. The experience affected him profoundly. 'It was a calm and beautiful spot. And I felt very grateful to be there, the guest of a people like mine who had endured foreign domination, he later wrote. 'When I stood there in prayer, I experienced great sadness for not being able to meet him (the Mahatma) in person. I wished that if I met him, I would touch his feet and bow down to him and ask the solution how to deal with China. But I also felt great joy at the magnificent example of his life. To me, he remains the model politician, a man who put his belief in altruism above all personal considerations and consistently maintained respect for all great spiritual traditions.'

Delhi Stay

The next few days in Delhi were occupied with official receptions at which the Dalai Lama was greeted by almost every dignitary in the capital. For the Dalai Lama was not only still nominally a head of state but also something more than a mere political figure. For most Indians he was an avatar, a holy man. Even though many did not share his religion, they eagerly sought darshan of him. The Dalai Lama met the President, Dr Radhakrishnan, and Vice President, Dr Rajendra Prasad, too. During his stay in Delhi, Zhou-en Lai, the Chinese Prime Minister, rushed to meet Prime Minister Nehru to ensure that the Dalai Lama returned to Tibet. The Chinese feared that he might be planning not to. They warned India against providing asylum to the young leader, calling it an 'unfriendly act' towards the Chinese.

45

India Tour

The Dalai Lama's visit to India was scheduled for eleven weeks. He was keen on visiting the sacred Buddhist sites. He visited the ruins of the once-famous university at Nalanda, where great masters such as Asanga and Shantideva taught. At Sarnath, he met members of the Mahabodhi Society, an organization established to encourage Buddhist studies, at the stupa in the Deer Park where the Buddha first taught the Dharma. He visited Varanasi too, spending time at the famous ghats by the holy Ganga. He also visited Vulture/Eagle Peak in Rajgir, Bihar, where the Buddha taught the Transcendent Wisdom Sutras, a collection of canonical Buddhist teachings that talk about how one needs to eliminate all attachments in order to find one's true self. It is considered the favourite retreat of the Buddha. Here, the Dalai Lama had a vision of monks reciting the Wisdom Mantra while vultures circled above, clearly an indication of the impermanence of life.

Visit to Bodh Gaya

The Dalai Lama travelled to Bodh Gaya, where he spent several days conducting ceremonies. He had been invited by the Indian government to the ceremonies that had been planned to commemorate the 2500th anniversary of the enlightenment of the Buddha. In a speech he made there, he noted that in one of the sutras, or scriptures, there is a prophecy made by the Buddha that 2500 years after his *parinirvana*—or passing beyond suffering—the dharma would flourish in the land of the red-faced people. He explained that while some scholars felt that it referred to its spread in Tibet, according to him it would be Europe.

47

A Sudden Meeting

On the last day of his stay at Bodh Gaya, unexpected summons came from the Chinese Embassy—Zhou-en Lai wanted an urgent meeting with the Tibetan leader in Delhi. At the meeting, Zhou-en Lai was very reassuring and even apologized for the actions of some of the Chinese officials. He repeated Mao's promise made to the Dalai Lama in Beijing that Tibet would have their real autonomy as soon as the Tibetans could manage their own country. He showed concern over the troubles in Lhasa and the various uprisings against the Chinese. But, most importantly, he spoke of the rumour that the Dalai Lama was not planning to return to Tibet. Even though Nehru advised the Dalai Lama to return to Tibet, his elder brothers, former Prime Minister Lukhangwa, among many others, advised him to stay in India and seek asylum. The situation in Tibet was not safe for the Dalai Lama to return.

To Stay in India or Return?

The dilemma in the Dalai Lama's mind was whether this was the right time to seek asylum in India. His second-eldest brother, Gyalo Thondup, was already in India. And his eldest brother, Thubten Jigme Norbu, had flown down to India from America specially to meet him. Both his brothers were in favour of the Dalai Lama staying in India. 'Their views really shook me,' he recalled later. Phala Thupten Woden, the Lord Chamberlain of Tibet and the Chief Secretary to the Dalai Lama, took a similar line. On the other hand, four members of the Governing Council of Tibet and his two tutors, Ling Rinpoche and Trijang Rinpoche, were all firmly in favour of him returning to Tibet. The Dalai Lama had to also think about the plight of the people of Tibet, who would be lost and bereaved without him.

49 Return to Tibet

On his way back to Tibet, the Dalai Lama stopped in Kalimpong, where he conducted sessions on the foundational tenets of Buddhism for his followers there. His brothers Taktser Rinpoche and Gyalo Thondup were in Kalimpong, too. They informed their brother that they would not return to Tibet. They wanted the Dalai Lama's support to liberate Tibet from the Chinese and hence wanted him to stay back in India, to help garner support from around the world. But the Dalai Lama was not going to change his views on violence as he did not believe that a guerrilla war would achieve anything. He decided to return to Tibet as he felt that as the leader of the Tibetan people, he should make one more attempt at peace. His brothers realized that they would have to continue the resistance. But when the Dalai Lama returned to Tibet, he was deeply saddened. The reassuring sights of the colourful Tibetan prayer flags all across his country had been replaced by red Chinese flags fluttering in the wind.

A Suspicious Invitation

In March 1959, while the *Monlam* Festival of the New Year was in full swing, some Chinese officials came to meet the Dalai Lama with a message from General Tan Kuan-sen. They, in fact, bore an invitation. When brought before the Dalai Lama at the Jokhang Temple, they elaborated that a new dance troupe had come from Beijing and the general would like to invite him to watch their wonderful performance. It seemed very suspicious. The Dalai Lama diplomatically declined, saying that he needed to attend to the ongoing New Year celebrations. He also mentioned that he was preparing for the final examination for the *Geshe Lharampa*, the highest academic degree of Tibetan Buddhism studies. He said he would give them a date once the festivities and exams were over. Obviously, the general was not happy with the Dalai Lama's reply.

51

The Final Exam

The curriculum, derived from the Nalanda tradition, consisted of five major and five minor subjects. The major subjects included logic, fine arts, Sanskrit grammar, medicine and Buddhist philosophy. The five minor subjects included poetry, drama, astrology, composition and synonyms. During the summer of 1958, at the age of twenty-three, the Dalai Lama took examinations from abbots or head monks of the monasteries of Drepung, Sera and Ganden. And the next year, in March 1959, he sat for his final examination in Jokhang Temple. Surrounded by thousands of monks, he engaged in a debate with thirty learned lamas for an entire day. He passed with honours and was awarded the *Geshe Lharampa* degree, the highest scholastic achievement. Most lamas took this examination when they were forty or more, but it was just as well that the Dalai Lama cleared his examinations when he did because the situation in Lhasa only got worse.

A Second Invitation

Meanwhile, General Tan Kuan-sen did not wait for long. He sent two of his officers to meet the chief abbot to convey yet another invitation on 7 March 1959, insisting on a specific date for the same dance performance by the troupe. The date was finalized for 10 March 1959. Two days later, the commander of the Dalai Lama's bodyguards, Kusung Depon, was called to the Chinese camp and was informed that the performance would be held at the barricaded military headquarters and no soldiers would be allowed to go with the Dalai Lama. Only two or three unarmed bodyguards would be allowed. At the Norbulingka Palace, there was fear and confusion. The Dalai Lama felt that if he did not accept the second invitation, it would be a breach of diplomacy. The others at the palace suspected that it was a trap, akin to what had been laid many times by the Chinese on Lamas from other monasteries.

53

A General's Ultimatum

On 10 March 1959, the people of Lhasa, fearing the worst, surrounded the Norbulingka Palace, to appeal to their leader to not leave the safety of his palace. While the Dalai Lama was in the garden of the palace, he was informed of trouble at the gate. More than 30,000 people had gathered outside, begging him to not go. There were shouts of protest, pleas to stay back. General Kuan-sen was livid with rage when he was informed that the Dalai Lama would not leave his palace. He announced that the Dalai Lama was to be present at their military headquarters at once and threatened that, if he did not, the consequences would be very grave. More Chinese troops could be seen in the hills all around the palace. But the protests continued and the women of Lhasa joined in too. Tibetan soldiers set fire to the uniforms that the Chinese were forcing them to wear. Public meetings were held all across Lhasa. 'Tibet is for Tibetans' became the rallying cry. The 10th March Uprising is annually commemorated by Tibetans all over the world.

The Enormous Decision

Since the Dalai Lama knew that the Chinese army could invade at any moment, he had no choice but to escape. But when was the right time to leave Tibet? For three months, he had waited patiently for a cue from Nechung Oracle, but he would say, 'Not yet, wait.' In the afternoon of 17 March 1959, Nechung went into a trance and told the Dalai Lama, 'Please leave tonight.' His body shook fervently and tears poured from his eyes incessantly. The Dalai Lama knew what he had to do now. He visited the temple of Mahakala for the last time and left a white khatag there as a sign that he would return. Did the young Dalai Lama think he ever would?

55

The Great Escape

A few minutes before ten o'clock on the night of 17 March 1959, the Dalai Lama rolled up his personal painting of Palden Lhamo (the protective goddess of the Dalai Lama and Lhasa), changed into the uniform of a Tibetan soldier with a rifle in his hand as a disguise, wore a cap, removed his iconic spectacles and walked out of Norbulingka Palace, his home, into the crowds outside, accompanied only by his bodyguards. In a video interview much later, he laughingly recalled just how heavy the rifle was to carry. The small group quietly slipped past the massive crowd and rode swiftly towards the Kyichu River, leaving Lhasa far behind. The journey to India and freedom had begun.

Last Glimpse of Lhasa

A few yak-skinned boats (coracles) awaited them on the banks of the Kyichu River. A tense journey across the river followed as searchlights from a Chinese camp beamed all around the area. The Dalai Lama was reunited with his immediate family, who had left in advance from the palace. A group of Tibetan soldiers were already at hand to ensure safe passage across Tibet, into India. And then, at a 16,000-foot pass in the mountains, Lhasa could be spotted, away in the distance. The Dalai Lama took one last look—would he ever come back to his beloved palace? Would he ever be allowed to? There was no time to think. As the leader and spiritual head of his people, he had to get out of his beloved Tibet if he was to stay alive to lead them.

57

The Arduous Journey

The group of hundred, travelling with the Dalai Lama, moved towards the Che-la Pass in the Tibetan mountains on mules and ponies. The weather was biting cold and their hands got numb. At some places, they had to cross snow-covered paths. They travelled during the night sometimes, to avoid being spotted by Chinese aircraft. Suddenly, an old man called Tashi Norbu joined the group and gifted the Dalai Lama a white horse, almost as if he knew that the mules and ponies were exhausted. It was a propitious sign. The group made its way down the steep slopes of sand and, after about three or four hours, came down to the ground level of Tsangpo River flowing through the Tibetan Plateau. A ferry was taken across the Tsangpo River and the group reached Kyishong valley. After crossing the river, they found a large crowd of Khampa warriors (a strong resistance group employing guerilla warfare against the invading Chinese army) who had gathered to greet the group.

The Horror at Norbulingka

After about a week of travelling through the steep mountains, news reached the Dalai Lama's party that Lhasa was bombarded and the Norbulingka Palace had been bombed on the morning of 20 March, three days after the Dalai Lama had left it on 17 March 1959. The Chinese entered Norbulingka and checked from corpse to corpse looking for the Dalai Lama. When they didn't find him, the Chinese realized that he had escaped. Many buildings, monasteries and homes had been destroyed, too. Monks were tortured and executed. Even the Potala Palace had not been spared. On 28 March, the Dalai Lama listened as Zhou-en Lai announced the annexation of Tibet to China. He knew that the Chinese would try and find him wherever he stayed in Tibet. Going into exile was the only option now.

On the Move

The group of people along with the Dalai Lama, growing larger and larger each day, plodded on, weary and scared. Through the mountains they crawled, constantly expecting the Chinese to catch up with them. The sudden appearance of an aircraft sent panic through the crowd. On the twelfth day of the long journey, the group arrived at Mangmang, the very last Tibetan settlement, before the Indian border. The Dalai Lama later recalled the extremely harrowing and difficult experience of his escape: 'Being a refugee is really a desperate, dangerous situation . . . When I left the Norbulingka, there was danger. We were passing very near the Chinese military barracks. It was just on the other side of the river, the Chinese check post there. You see, we had definite information two or three weeks before I left, that the Chinese were fully prepared to attack us. It was only a question of the day and hour.'

The Last Stop in Tibet

After reaching Lhuntze Dzong, still in Tibet, the Dalai Lama formally repudiated the Seventeen-Point Agreement and announced the formation of his interim government. While at the monastery at Lhuntze Dzong, a small group of the fittest men in his party was sent ahead to seek asylum in India. The Dalai Lama's earlier visit to India had been a very welcoming one. Prime Minister Nehru had been very hospitable and warm as had all the other people he had interacted with during his eleven-week stay. But this time, he was fleeing from communist China's rule. The lives of so many who were fleeing with the Dalai Lama were also at stake, based on India's reaction; but on their arrival at Mamgmang, the messengers who had been sent in advance to the Indian border had returned with the good news that the Indian government had granted asylum to him and his group. What a relief that was for the Dalai Lama!

61

The Dalai Lama Falls Ill

The Dalai Lama was exhausted. The party had encountered a blizzard the previous day and witnessed incessant rainfall. On the thirteenth day of their journey towards the Indo-Tibetan border, the Dalai Lama woke up with a fever. He was delirious and could barely get up. His mother nursed him while he rested in a dry loft above a stable. They were all still camped in Mangmang. There was only one day's travel left to reach the Indo-Tibetan border. On the radio he heard about himself. There were rumours that he had fallen off a horse and badly injured himself. The Dalai Lama needed to recover, but the news that the Chinese were closing in on them did not allow for that.

India at Last

The Dalai Lama's perilous journey to asylum was drawing to a close. The group had made their way across the arduous Himalayan region on pony-back, yak-back and on foot. They had even crossed the wide Brahmaputra River. At Mangmang, their last halt, a crucial decision had to be taken. The entire party could not cross into India. It was finally decided that the monks and the government officials would go across the border with the Dalai Lama and his family, while the Tibetan soldiers and the guerilla fighters opted to stay back. The Dalai Lama was profoundly moved by the patriotism of these men, more so because he knew that there was a very slim chance that any of them would survive the Chinese attacks. Two exhausting weeks had passed. The Dalai Lama and his entourage finally reached the Indian border at Khenzimane (demarcates the frontier in the Chuthangmu area) on 31 March 1959.

63

Preparations at the Border

Having received information about the possibility of the Dalai Lama seeking entry into India, T.S. Murthy, Assistant Political Officer (APO), Tawang, reached Chuthangmu to receive the party on 31 March 1959. So, when the Dalai Lama and his party reached, he was received warmly by Mr Murthy. Two days later, his party reached Lumla, where they were met by Har Mander Singh, the Political Officer (PO), Tawang. A day later, the Dalai Lama was given a guard of honour by the Assam Rifles. Here, he finally got to rest. Every time subsequently that he has visited the Tawang area (in Arunachal Pradesh), it has always been very emotional. For, he recalls his escape in 1959, when it was at these very Northeastern hills that he had got his first taste of freedom. From Tawang, they went to Bomdila, where a telegram of welcome from Prime Minister Nehru awaited the Dalai Lama. It assured the spiritual ruler of the Tibetan people that he was welcome to reside in India with his family and his entourage.

Reception at Tezpur

On 18 April 1959, the Indian government sent many jeeps to Bomdila to bring the party to Tezpur. There the press and many devotees were eagerly waiting for the Dalai Lama. When he appeared before them, looking well rested, the relief, excitement and joy, especially among the Tibetan expatriates, was palpable. Everyone waited for a glimpse or a word from the Dalai Lama. But he was overwhelmed with gratitude and did not say a word. A statement of his was read to the crowd, stating that he had come to India by his own free will (the Chinese had announced that he had been abducted) and that he hoped that there would be no more bloodshed in Tibet. Then the Dalai Lama, his family and the rest of his party boarded a special train to Mussoorie. All along the way, at every station, his followers thronged the platforms. As a temporary, immediate requirement, the India government had provided Birla House in Mussoorie for the Dalai Lama. This is where his period of exile began.

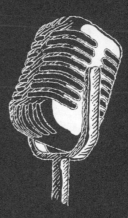

65

Meeting with Nehru

One of the Dalai Lama's first official visitors in Mussoorie was Prime Minister Nehru, who arrived at his residence on 24 April 1959 on a white horse, promising him all the help he needed in his country. On 8 September 1959, the Dalai Lama visited the Prime Minister and his daughter Indira Gandhi in Delhi. In June that year, the Dalai Lama had spoken about the atrocities committed by the Chinese in Tibet at a press conference and called for an international commission to probe into the Chinese acts of brutality. The Dalai Lama had several helpful meetings with Nehru and the Prime Minister felt that he should focus on preserving the Tibetan culture and educating the children but was not prepared to recognize the Dalai Lama's government in exile and was also not particularly encouraging of the need to have the Tibetan issue discussed at the United Nations. Though he assured that India would always be sympathetic to the Dalai Lama's cause and people, he could not afford to antagonize China.

Pilgrimage to Bodh Gaya

On 25 January 1960, the Dalai Lama embarked on a pilgrimage to Bodh Gaya and stayed until 14 February. He was residing in Mussoorie at the time. He was probably looking for solace and courage for himself and his suffering followers. He conducted some special Tibetan ceremonies here at the holiest of holy Buddhist spots, where a visit by the Fourteenth Dalai Lama, now in exile, was a big draw to the small town. Besides Buddhists, many more thronged to Bodh Gaya to listen to the Dalai Lama, who now lived, studied and taught in their country. For the Buddhists, there was no better teacher than the Dalai Lama.

67 Parliament-in-Exile

While in Bodh Gaya, in February 1960, the Dalai Lama outlined a detailed programme of democratic practice for exiled Tibetans. This was something that he had wanted to do much earlier. Tibetans had had no experience of democracy prior to this. For the Tibetan Parliament-in-Exile (TPiE), he advised them to set up an elected body with three exiled representatives from the three provinces in Tibet (Amdo, Kham and U-Tsang), and one each from the four religious schools of Tibetan Buddhism. After elections were held, thirteen elected representatives, known as Deputies, were designated as the Commission of Tibetan People's Deputies (CTPD), who took oath of office on 2 September 1960. From 1975 onwards, this date has been observed as Tibetan Democracy Day. Members of the Seventeenth Tibetan Parliament-in-Exile were sworn in on 8 October 2021.

A New Home at Dharamsala

On his return to Mussoorie from Bodh Gaya, the Dalai Lama was taken aback to learn that the Indian government had decided to relocate him to a quaint little place called Dharamsala in Himachal Pradesh. Not knowing where exactly it was, he looked for it on a map. Since it was a remote hill-station that was not very well connected, the Dalai Lama felt that the relocation may prove to be an obstacle. He requested that he be allowed to send a member of the *Kashag*, the governing council, to Dharamsala on a recce. W.G. Kundeling visited Dharamsala and returned after a week. 'Dharamsala's water is better than Mussoorie milk,' he reported. And so, on 29 April 1960, the Dalai Lama travelled by train to Pathankot in Punjab and then to Dharamsala by road. Along the long, winding hill-roads that led up to the village of McLeod Ganj, he vividly remembers the beautiful countryside he traversed to find his new home.

69

The Newborn Baby Bird

Dharamsala is home to wild monkeys, and many of them live around the Dalai Lama's residence as well. One day, the Dalai Lama noticed some wild monkeys harassing a baby bird in a tree. He immediately called his bodyguards and told them, 'You don't have to worry about my safety. But you can watch this newborn baby bird and make sure it's safe from the wild monkeys.' His bodyguards stood at the foot of the tree for several days and kept a watch on the bird till it was old enough to fly.

A Purr-fect Friend

Once, the Dalai Lama found a stray cat in his garden and named it Tsering. Tsering was the most ideal pet there could be—she was loving, obedient and loyal. But she had one flaw—she couldn't resist chasing mice. And her master could not bear to see her kill a helpless creature. One day, when the Dalai Lama caught Tsering chasing a mouse, he ran after her. Tsering realized that she'd done something wrong and climbed up a curtain but lost her balance and fell down, badly injuring her leg. The Dalai Lama was full of remorse. He tended to Tsering but she could not recover from the injury and died in a few days. A couple of weeks later, the Dalai Lama heard a pitiful cry from the garden. He went out to find a small kitten lying in the bushes. And guess what—the kitten was crippled exactly as Tsering had been! The Dalai Lama took her inside and took great care of her.

Food Habits

The Dalai Lama noted that the monastic principles of Buddhism in general do not prohibit meat-eating. For the monks are neither vegetarian nor non-vegetarian—they must accept whatever is offered to them. But the monastic principles also clearly mention that animals specifically slaughtered to feed the monks should not be eaten. When the Dalai Lama took residence in India, which has a rich tradition of vegetarianism, he adopted a vegetarian diet. But after twenty months, he developed a gall bladder condition and contracted a Hepatitis B infection. That was when he was encouraged by his doctors to get back to a non-vegetarian diet to aid his recovery. In recent years though, he has been actively encouraging vegetarianism. The Dalai Lama also emphasizes that it would be impractical to suggest that everyone becomes vegetarian, especially in cold climate regions like northern Tibet and Mongolia. But countries like India have a rich supply of vegetables and are known for vegetarianism.

Can a Monk Feel Sad?

The Dalai Lama always says that though he is a Buddhist monk who began his serious Buddhist study at the age of six and does his meditation practice five to six hours a day even today, he is also a human being with feelings. So, he does get angry and sad like everyone else. When he feels sad, he often visualizes the Buddha in the lotus position and himself sitting at his feet. Then, he imagines resting his head on the Buddha's left knee. This, His Holiness says, always eases his sadness and comforts him.

73 Compassion and Happiness

The Dalai Lama believes that as human beings what we all have in common is a wish, at the very core of our hearts, to be happy. But we are always trying to improve our academics, and we don't think too much about being better persons. He says that being a more compassionate and warm-hearted person can result in peace of mind. In a globalized, interdependent world, it is particularly important to nurture compassion. The destruction of the enemy would be the destruction of one's own self.

A Forced Friendship

The Dalai Lama once told a story from when he was 'a young, naughty Dalai Lama' and enviously watched his teacher feed a parrot some nuts. As the parrot nibbled from the teacher's fingers, the teacher stroked its head, at which the bird appeared to enter a state of ecstasy. Hoping to attain the same kind of affection from the parrot, the ten-year-old Dalai Lama grabbed some seeds to feed the bird. The parrot took the food very aggressively, and when the young Dalai Lama tried to touch it, the parrot began to bite him. So, the Dalai Lama took a small stick and hit the bird. The prospect of friendship between the Dalai Lama and the parrot was over. But from this incident the Dalai Lama learnt a very good lesson in how to make friends: not by force but by compassion.

75

A Grave Loss

In 1983, Ling Rinpoche, the Dalai Lama's principal teacher, passed away. The Dalai Lama felt that he had lost a strong rock that he always leaned on. Rinpoche was extremely weak in the months leading to his death, and the Dalai Lama believed that he lived those extra months only to give him the time he needed to prepare for a life without his loving teacher. Even after his death, Rinpoche's body did not decay for thirteen days despite the hot Indian weather. The Dalai Lama says that he has no doubt that this, too, was his doing as he wanted him to come to terms with his passing. So, rather than mourning his death, the Dalai Lama decided to focus his energy on serving others in order to follow his beloved teacher's principles.

The Four Commitments

The Dalai Lama then decided to dedicate his life towards four major commitments. The first was his commitment as a human being. Helping people enhances the value of care, compassion, forgiveness, tolerance, contentment, self-discipline and hope in the world. His second commitment was to encourage harmony between the world's various religious traditions. As a Buddhist practitioner, he wished for mutual understanding between all the major religions. He believed that every religion has the capacity to serve humanity and we should respect them all, since all aspire to foster compassion. His third commitment was to preserve the Tibetan identity and culture and to protect the Tibetan environment. His fourth commitment was to revive the ancient Indian knowledge traditions of how to achieve inner peace and happiness.

The Nobel Peace Prize

In 1989, His Holiness the Fourteenth Dalai Lama was awarded the Nobel Peace Prize for advocating 'peaceful solutions based upon tolerance and mutual respect in order to preserve the historical and cultural heritage of his people.' In his acceptance speech, he said, 'I feel honoured, humbled and deeply moved that you should give this important prize to a simple monk from Tibet; I am no one special. But I believe the prize is a recognition of the true value of altruism, love, compassion and non-violence, which I try to practise, in accordance with the teachings of the Buddha and the great sages of India and Tibet . . . I accept the prize with profound gratitude on behalf of the oppressed everywhere, and for all those who struggle for freedom and work for world peace.'

After the Win

After the Dalai Lama won the Nobel Peace Prize in 1989, there were many Tibetans and admirers who had gathered outside the Grand Hotel in Oslo, Norway, for the torchlight procession—a parade that starts at Oslo Central Station and ends in front of the Grand Hotel in honour of the Nobel Peace Prize laureates. They hoped to catch a glimpse of their spiritual leader. While they all waited eagerly, the Dalai Lama came out of the balcony of the Nobel Suite and waved to everyone below. The crowd waved their precious Tibetan flags jubilantly. But soon, the Dalai Lama went back in, much to the disappointment of the large crowd. Suddenly he reappeared, this time among all his followers and

admirers, waving the Tibetan flag along with them. It was a memorable experience for those who were present.

79

The Middle Way Approach

The Middle Way Approach was proposed by the Dalai Lama to peacefully resolve the issue between Tibet and China. Through a series of discussions, the Central Tibetan Administration decided that the Tibetan people would not accept the present status of Tibet under the People's Republic of China, but they would not seek independence for Tibet either. Treading a path in-between would mean genuine autonomy for all Tibetans living in the three traditional provinces of Tibet within the framework of the People's Republic of China. This meant that for Tibetans, the protection and preservation of their culture, religion and national identity would be of utmost importance. A four-day conference was organized in Dharamsala from 6 June 1988, where the Middle Way Approach was endorsed unanimously. Thereafter, the Dalai Lama issued a statement in the European parliament in Strasbourg on 15 June 1988, but the Chinese government did not respond positively to the proposal. The Dalai Lama proposed it again in 1996 and 1997.

His Holiness and the Mahatma

The Dalai Lama is one of the foremost disciples of the Mahatma and believes that he took the three-thousand-year-old tradition of *ahimsa* (non-violence) and *karuna* (compassion) and made it something living and relevant. In 1989, while accepting the Nobel Peace Prize in Oslo, the Dalai Lama said, 'It is a tribute to the man who founded the modern tradition of non-violent action for change, Mahatma Gandhi, whose life taught and inspired me.' On one occasion, during his winter stay in the Potala Palace, Mahatma Gandhi appeared in the Dalai Lama's dream. 'Not like the pictures, but Gandhi for real,' he said while narrating the experience. When asked what he would like to say to the Mahatma if he met him today, the Dalai Lama replied, 'I very much want to meet him, and first, touch his feet. Then, I think he may have some idea about how to deal with China.' Saying this, the Dalai Lama threw back his head laughing.

81

Dialogues with Scientists

Science and technology fascinated the Dalai Lama right from his childhood. He always wanted to have open discussions with scientists from all over the world. He met the quantum physicist David Bohm in 1979 in Europe. They immediately built a rapport and had several meetings over the years. The Dalai Lama credits Bohm for explaining to him many scientific concepts. Another scientist with whom he developed a close association was Carl Friedrich von Weizaäcker, who discussed quantum physics and empiricism, or practical experience as the basis of knowledge, with the Dalai Lama. The German physicist later observed that the Buddhist understanding of empiricism is broader than that of modern science because it includes the meditative states as well. The Dalai Lama also enjoyed a deep connection with astrophysicist Carl Sagan and discussed religion, consciousness and science with him.

Science and Spirituality

The Dalai Lama started interacting with scientists out of his own curiosity, but when it became clear that these could be of great value to the Buddhists who are already familiar with the workings of the inner world to learn more about physical reality, the Dalai Lama thought of opening these dialogues up for the monks. In 1987, the Dalai Lama met the neuroscientist Francisco Varela and businessmen Adam Engle. They convened a week-long discussion between various scientists and the Dalai Lama in Dharamsala. From this grew the Mind & Life Institute that has, over the last thirty years, held thirty-three of these landmark dialogues. In 1998, the Emory-Tibet partnership was founded, which has implemented modern science education into the curriculum of monastic institutions. In 2012, the Dalai Lama won the prestigious Templeton Prize to honour his contribution in harnessing the power of science to explore the deepest questions of the universe and humankind's place and purpose in it.

83

Sense of Humour

Once, the Dalai Lama was presiding over a symposium on 'How to bridge science and Buddhism for mutual enrichment'. Many renowned scientists, monks, nuns and interested followers had gathered for the symposium, looking as serious as the topic. The Dalai Lama walked in, smiling and waving at the people who'd gathered to listen to him. He sat down on the chair and took the white washcloth on the table in front of him to wipe the sweat on his brow. He then put the cloth on his head, like a floppy little hat. Then, he reached for a glass jar of candy on the table. 'This is not decoration,' he joked, holding it up. He pointed to himself and said, 'eat', and then popped the candy into his mouth. His childlike behaviour, laughing and joking, did the trick. The sombre crowd began laughing with him. When one of his colleagues later asked the Dalai Lama about why he decided to wear the washcloth so comically, he said that he is practical and gets hot. But he also hinted at something deeper: It's important for leaders, particularly spiritual leaders, to 'act like a human being'.

Emotional Hygiene

On many occasions, the Dalai Lama has spoken about how children do not care about the differences in faith, family or nationality—they just play with their companions. But as we grow up, the secondary differences corrode our mind and we start to function less humanly. Based on these differences, we pit 'us' against 'them', which lays the ground for all kinds of conflicts. What we need to do is teach children 'emotional hygiene'—a way to tackle their destructive emotions—just as they are taught physical hygiene. The Dalai Lama invited Emory University, Atlanta, Georgia, to create such a programme. The result was the SEE (Social, Emotional and Ethical) Learning, an innovative kindergarten to graduation programme. It is available in twelve languages and is implemented in many schools in India, the US and European countries.

85

The Dalai Lama's Hero

In 2001, the Dalai Lama met Richard Moore, a businessman, musician and the founder of Children in Crossfire, a charitable organization that works with underprivileged children in Tanzania, Gambia, Ethiopia and Derry (Ireland). It was a public event where Richard recounted the moving story of his life. In 1972, Richard was blinded by a rubber bullet fired at close range into his face by a British soldier during a conflict in Northern Ireland. Not only did he accept his fate but after meeting the soldier who shot him, he also befriended him. The Dalai Lama, on meeting him, told him, 'Whether you believe it or not, you are my hero and a wonderful son of humanity. Despite your tremendously painful experience, you don't have any anger or hate. You accept what has happened and keep your peace of mind. You are a good example and model.'

Bonding with Archbishop Tutu

The Dalai Lama and the South African freedom-fighter and archbishop, Desmund Tutu, were not just two of the world's best-known spiritual leaders but also dear friends. It was a friendship rooted in the burden both men carried as world leaders, dedicated to bringing justice to their communities. In 2009, when His Holiness and the archbishop both received the Spiritual Leadership Award, the archbishop was asked to say something about the Dalai Lama. 'He has an incredible serenity,' he said. 'Imagine, I mean, we praise (former South African President and earlier anti-apartheid activist) Nelson Mandela—and we do, quite rightly—for twenty-seven years in jail and coming out with that magnanimity. But the Dalai Lama has been in exile for fifty years and you'd have expected that, by now, he would have been corroded by a bitterness. But he hasn't.' And then, jokingly, he added, 'He's actually quite mischievous.'

87

Spiritual Brothers

The Dalai Lama often narrated a story about how as a small boy in Tibet, he felt that his own religion must be the best—and that other faiths were somehow inferior. But he realized how naive he was, and how dangerous the extremes of religious intolerance can be. An early eye-opener for him was meeting the Trappist monk (a religious order of monks in the Roman Catholic Church), Thomas Merton, in India shortly before the monk's untimely death in 1968. Merton told him that he could be perfectly faithful to Christianity, yet learn from other religions like Buddhism. An important point in their discussion was how compassion was a strong, unifying thread among all the major faiths. The Dalai Lama said that finding common ground among faiths can help us bridge needless divides at a time when unified action is more crucial than ever. As a collective, we must embrace the oneness of humanity as we face global issues such as economic crises and climate change. At that scale, our response must be as one.

The Son of India

The Dalai Lama's presence in India, which the 1962 war made irreversible, is a constant strain on Sino-Indian relations. His Holiness is more than aware of this. His gratitude to India is a debt he bears all the time. He was fully aware that for Beijing, the Dalai Lama's government-in-exile in Dharamsala had been a constant challenge to its rule in Tibet. The Dalai Lama has always praised India's role in ensuring freedom and safety for the Tibetan refugees who have been living in exile in the country since the Chinese takeover of Tibet in 1950. As the Dalai Lama once said, 'I consider myself as the son of India. Every part of my brain is filled with ancient Indian knowledge and this physical body is because of Indian dal and rice.'

Baba Amte

A noted humanitarian activist and Gandhian, Baba Amte set up Anandvan, an ashram in Chandrapur, Maharashtra, for those suffering from leprosy. He slowly turned the barren land into a thriving settlement with the help of the leprosy patients. Baba Amte's admirers included the Dalai Lama, who described his work as 'practical compassion, real transformation and the proper way to develop India'. The Dalai Lama visited Baba Amte in 1990 and was touched by the work that he saw him doing there. He stayed with Baba Amte and was shown around the colony. At the end of the tour, both men were moved to tears. The Dalai Lama mourned the demise of Baba Amte on 11 February 2008. He was ninety-four at the time of his death. In his condolence message to Baba Amte's two sons, Vikas and Prakash, the Dalai Lama wrote, 'At the time I could not help feeling that here was someone who was truly compassionate. In fact, I told him at the time that whereas my compassion is just so much talk, his shone through everything he did, including his work for creating greater awareness about the protection of our environment.'

Meeting Mother Teresa

The Dalai Lama met Mother Teresa for the first time at the Global Survival Conference in Christ Church, Oxford University (11–15 April 1988). After meeting her, he often told Buddhist monks and nuns to follow the example of Mother Teresa and serve the poorest of the poor. The Dalai Lama lit a candle at the mausoleum of Mother Teresa during his visit to Kolkata in 2015. Writing to the Mother Superior of the Missionaries of Charity (the Order founded by Mother Teresa), the Dalai Lama expressed delight that the Pope had proclaimed Mother Teresa a saint the following year: 'I rejoice at this recognition as an admirer of her dedicated service to humanity, particularly the way she cared for the poorest of the poor. I join you in celebrating her extraordinary life. Meeting Mother Teresa, it was clear she was an exemplary person . . . She revealed the true practice of love in her charitable activities. Although she is no longer physically with us, her spirit lives on in the work you all do.'

91

Ending a 369-year-old Tradition

In 2011, the Dalai Lama announced that he would end the 369-year-old *Gaden Phodrang* system of governance, which had made him both political and spiritual leader. He wished to devolve political powers to an elected prime minister. The first Tibetan prime minister-in-exile was elected and the Dalai Lama formally announced his semi-retirement. He declared: 'One-man rule is both anachronistic and undesirable . . . In order for our democratization to be complete, the time has come for me to devolve my formal authority . . . it is necessary . . . in order that the Tibetan administration can become self-reliant rather than being dependent on the Dalai Lama.' Many people appealed to the Dalai Lama to reconsider his decision, but he stressed his commitment to democracy and how Tibetans needed a leader elected by the Tibetan people. Since then, the Dalai Lama has been working tirelessly towards the wider issues concerning the whole of humanity.

The *Geshema* Degree

The 1980s were marked by the arrival of hundreds of exiled Tibetan monks and nuns in Dharamsala. One of the first decisions taken by the Tibetan government-in-exile was to set up centres of learning. Making a bold move then, the Dalai Lama suggested that the Tibetan Buddhist schools could start granting nuns access to higher philosophical studies, training them as *geshemas* (a female form of the Tibetan Buddhist academic degree *geshe*). At first, this idea generated resistance, but the Dalai Lama was firm in his commitment. In 1995, the first inter-nunnery debating competition was organized. Impressed by the level of excellence of their philosophical debates, the Dalai Lama suggested in 2012 that the nuns of the Gelugpa (one of the four major schools of Tibetan Buddhism) tradition should be able to take the *geshe* examination. On 22 December 2016, twenty happy nuns, from six nunneries in India and Nepal, received their *geshema* degree, beginning a historic chapter in Tibetan Buddhism.

93

The Many Tenzins

According to the Tibetan traditions, when a child is born, the parents usually approach a lama to name him. Most Tibetans do not have a surname or a family name. Tibetans also change their names at various important junctures of their lives, such as marriage or after recovering from a serious illness. The Tibetans-in-exile have access to His Holiness the Dalai Lama and many parents go to him to name their newborns. The names that the Dalai Lama suggests, always start with Tenzin—which means 'the upholder of the Buddhist dharma' and comes from his own name, Tenzin Gyatso. Tenzin has therefore become the most common Tibetan name for Tibetans-in-exile and many girls and boys have Tenzin in their names.

The Next Dalai Lama . . .

His Holiness is regularly faced with the question of who the next Dalai Lama will be and how he would be chosen. He often tells this story of how a particularly persistent journalist once asked him about his reincarnation. The Dalai Lama took off his glasses, looked him in the eye and answered, 'Look at my face. Do you think there's any rush?' With the creation of the democratic government-in-exile, the Dalai Lama voluntarily took a step back from active politics in May 2011. He, on many occasions, has publicly suggested that the incarnation of Dalai Lama may end with him, since 'the institution has outlived its usefulness'.

95

'I Don't Know.'

The British-born Indian essayist and novelist, Pico Iyer, travelled extensively with the Dalai Lama. The one thing that the Dalai Lama said to people for reassurance and confidence was: 'I don't know.' When people asked him questions like, 'What's going to happen to Tibet?', 'When are we ever going to get world peace?' or 'What's the best way to raise children?', the Dalai Lama simply said, 'Frankly, I don't know.' This 'wisdom of ignorance' or 'learned ignorance', is at the centre of thinking of many philosophers, including Socrates. It is captured by the well-known statement: 'I know only one thing—that I know nothing.' The famous fifteenth-century German astronomer, mathematician and philosopher Nicholas of Cusa also placed a lot of importance in this idea.

A Super Accessible Leader

The Dalai Lama is one of the most accessible of world leaders. Web interactions, social media (the Dalai Lama's Twitter account has over nineteen million followers) and online updates are some of the ways through which he stays connected with the people across the world. Here are a few of the Dalai Lama's most liked tweets:

What we need today are universal values based not on faith but on scientific findings, common experience and common sense. (16 September 2017)

Times change and reality changes. In the past, social customs and cultural traditions may have held women back but modern times favour equality and education has brought equality of opportunity. Now is the time to change our old ways of thinking—gender, colour, no difference. (8 March 2022)

We share this one planet, our only home so we have to take better care of it. We must cultivate compassion not only for our fellow human beings, but also for the other animals, birds and insects with whom we share the world. Concern for others is necessary for our survival. (4 February 2022)

97

A Day in the Life of . . .

When the Dalai Lama is not travelling and is home in Dharamsala, he starts his day at around 3.30 a.m. After his morning shower, he prays and meditates for about two hours. He then takes a morning walk around the residential premises. Breakfast is served at 5.30 a.m. The Dalai Lama usually has porridge, tsampa (barley powder), bread and fruit preserves and tea for breakfast. During breakfast, he listens to BBC World News on his radio. Then, he continues his prayers and meditation. From around 9 a.m., the Dalai Lama studies Buddhist texts for a couple of hours. Lunch is served at 11.30 a.m. If some interviews or staff engagements are scheduled for him, he visits his office in the mornings. Upon his return, he has tea at around 4.30 p.m., followed by evening prayers and meditation. Following strict monastic rules, the Dalai Lama does not have dinner. He usually retires to bed at around 7 p.m.

Green Thumb

The Dalai Lama's love for nature manifests in his keen interest in gardening. Among his favourite places at his home in Dharamsala are his lush gardens, where he grows all sorts of plants. He also has greenhouses built at his residence where a variety of wildflowers are grown. He often brings cuttings from his many travels and also receives them as gifts. On his travels, he relishes his visits to botanical gardens, such as the Royal Botanical Gardens in Kew, London, and the Brindavan Gardens in Mysore. 'Planting and nurturing plants and trees are virtuous acts,' the Dalai Lama once wrote in an essay. The famous botanical artist Dianne Aigaki documented the rich flora in the Dalai Lama's gardens by creating detailed scientific paintings of the rare wildflowers. She spent many hours in the Dalai Lama's gardens to capture the beauty of the plants.

99

Our Environment, Our Home

One of the Dalai Lama's core principles is taking care of our planet. He believes that it's like looking after our own home, so it is our universal responsibility and an urgent one at that. From ordering measures for forest protection, banning hunting in erstwhile independent Tibet, ending poultry farming, promoting vegetarianism among the exiled Tibetan community in India, calling for tree plantation and wildlife protection and urging for global cooperation on climate change— the Dalai Lama has consistently worked for environmental conservation for the last decades. After the devolution of all political responsibility to a democratically elected leader of the Tibetan people in 2011, the Dalai Lama evocatively stated that he would continue to devote his life to the protection of the environment. This reaffirmed his lifelong objective of striving for environmental conservation. Such a significant pledge from the Dalai Lama immensely strengthens the cause of protecting our planet.

On the Pandemic

Owing to the pandemic, the Dalai Lama had spent several months in isolation. Since the beginning of the pandemic, however, he has, on several occasions, addressed the difficulties the world is facing through various online interactions. He extended his compassion and prayers to the Chinese people as well, despite the strained relations. In many of his addresses, the Dalai Lama has reiterated that science and compassion can together help us overcome this grave health crisis. In one of his interactions, he said, 'The spread of the virus demonstrates how the world is interdependent and how we all impact one another. But it also reminds us that a compassionate or constructive act—whether working in hospitals or just observing social distancing—has the potential to help many . . . No matter how difficult the situation may be, we should employ science and human ingenuity with determination and courage to overcome the problems that confront us.'

TRIVIA AND MORE

Timeline

1933   Thubten Gyatso, the Thirteenth Dalai Lama, passes away in Lhasa at the age of fifty-seven.

1935   Lhamo Thondup is born in Takster, Amdo, Tibet.

1938   A delegation of monks, looking for the new Dalai Lama, find Lhamo Thondup.

1939   Lhamo Thondup and his family depart from Amdo for a three-month journey to Lhasa. A public declaration of the recognition of the Fourteenth Dalai Lama is made.

1940   His Holiness the Fourteenth Dalai Lama's enthronement ceremony takes place in Lhasa, Tibet. His monastic education begins at the age of five.

1950   The Chinese soldiers of the People's Liberation Army invade Tibet.

1950   His Holiness the Fourteenth Dalai Lama assumes full political power as Tibetan Head of State and Government. He departs for Dromo because of Chinese threat.

1951 The Seventeen-Point Agreement is signed by a Tibetan delegation under duress in Beijing. The Dalai Lama arrives in Lhasa from Dromo.

1954 The Dalai Lama visits China for peace talks and meets Mao Zedong.

1956 The Dalai Lama makes his first trip to India to participate in the celebration of the 2500th anniversary of the Buddha's Enlightenment.

1959 The Dalai Lama passes the *Geshe Lharampa* degree with honours.

1959 Tibetans gather outside Norbulingka Palace to prevent the Dalai Lama from going to a performance at the Chinese Army Camp in Lhasa. An uprising erupts against the Chinese rule. The People's Republic of China intensifies its suppression.

1959 The Dalai Lama escapes from Norbulingka Palace at night. After a harrowing fourteen-day journey, His Holiness enters India.

1959 The Dalai Lama officially takes up temporary residence in exile in Mussoorie, India. He holds a press conference and formally repudiates the Seventeen-Point Agreement.

1960 Dharamsala, India, becomes home to the Dalai Lama and the headquarters of the government-in-exile of Tibet.

1963 His Holiness presents a draft constitution for Tibet. The first exile Tibetan parliament is established in Dharamsala.

1989 His Holiness the Fourteenth Dalai Lama is awarded the Nobel Peace Prize by Egil Aarvik, Chairman of the Nobel Committee.

2011 The Dalai Lama gives up his political powers.

2012 The Dalai Lama is awarded the Templeton Prize.

2020 Coinciding with his eighty-fifth birthday, the Dalai Lama releases an album of teaching and mantras accompanied by music titled 'Inner World'.

The Dalai Lamas

- First Dalai Lama: Gedun Drupa (1391–1474)
- Second Dalai Lama: Gedun Gyatso (1492–1542)
- Third Dalai Lama: Sonam Gyatso (1578–1588)
- Fourth Dalai Lama: Yonten Gyatso (1601–1617)
- Fifth Dalai Lama: Ngawang Lobsang Gyatso (1642–1682)
- Sixth Dalai Lama: Tsangyang Gyatso (1697–1706)
- Seventh Dalai Lama: Kelzang Gyatso (1720–1757)
- Eighth Dalai Lama: Jamphel Gyatso (1762–1804)
- Ninth Dalai Lama: Lungtok Gyatso (1810–1815)
- Tenth Dalai Lama: Tsultrim Gyatso (1826–1837)
- Eleventh Dalai Lama: Khedrup Gyatso (1842–1856)
- Twelfth Dalai Lama: Trinley Gyatso (1860–1875)
- Thirteenth Dalai Lama: Thubten Gyatso (1879–1933)
- Fourteenth Dalai Lama: Tenzin Gyatso (1950–present)

Books by the Dalai Lama

- *My Land and My People: The Original Autobiography of His Holiness the Dalai Lama of Tibet*
- *Freedom in Exile: The Autobiography of the Dalai Lama of Tibet*
- *My Spiritual Autobiography*
- *In My Own Words: An Introduction to My Teachings and Philosophy*
- *Love, Kindness and Universal Responsibility*
- *The Seed of Compassion: Lessons from the Life and Teachings of His Holiness the Dalai Lama*
- *This Fragile Planet: His Holiness the Dalai Lama on Environment*
- *Our Only Home: A Climate Appeal to the World*
- *The Universe in a Single Atom: The Convergence of Science and Spirituality*
- *A Simple Path*

Foundation of Universal Responsibility

'I believe that to meet the challenge of our times, human beings will have to develop a greater sense of universal responsibility. Each of us must learn to work not just for his or her own self, family or nation, but for the benefit of all mankind. Universal responsibility is the real key to human survival. It is the best foundation for world peace, the equitable use of natural resources, and through concern for future generations, the proper care of the environment. I, for one, truly believe that individuals can make a difference in society. Since periods of great change such as the present one come so rarely in human history, it is up to each of us to make the best use of our time to help create a happier world.'

—His Holiness the Fourteenth Dalai Lama

Founded in November, 1990, with the funds from the Nobel Peace Prize awarded to His Holiness in 1989, the Foundation for Universal Responsibility of His Holiness the Dalai Lama, is an organization that brings together people of different faiths, professions and nationalities, through a range of creative initiatives and mutually sustaining collaborations that seek to foster an inclusive, just and non-violent world. It also seeks to expand the network of globally committed citizens who are sensitive to responsibilities in an interdependent world.

Selected Bibliography

- Lama, The Dalai. *Freedom in Exile: The Autobiography of the Dalai Lama*. HarperOne, 2008
- Tethong, Tenzin Geyche. *His Holiness the Fourteenth Dalai Lama: An Illustrated Biography*. Roli Books, 2020
- Kimmel, Elizabeth Cody. B*oy on the Lion Throne: The Childhood of the 14th Dalai Lama*. Flash Point, 2009
- George, Charles. *The Dalai Lama (People in the News)*. Cengage Gale, 2009
- Norman, Alexander. *The Dalai Lama: An Extraordinary Life*. HarperCollins India, 2020
- Mehrotra, Rajiv (Editor). *Understanding the Dalai Lama*. Hay House, 2009
- Saiwai, Tetsu. *The 14th Dalai Lama: A Manga Biography*. Penguin Books, 2010
- Meyers, William and Thurman, Robert A.F., *Man of Peace: The Illustrated Life Story of the Dalai Lama of Tibet*, Tibet House US, 2017
- Anantharaman, Aravinda. *The 14th Dalai Lama: Buddha of Compassion*. Puffin Lives, 2011
- www.dalailama.com, accessed 25 May 2022
- Osnos, Evan. 'The Next Incarnation', *The New Yorker*. 2010
- *India Today*. August 2021